W9-CLD-358

LOOKING INTO THE
GRAND CANYON

BY MARTHA LONDON

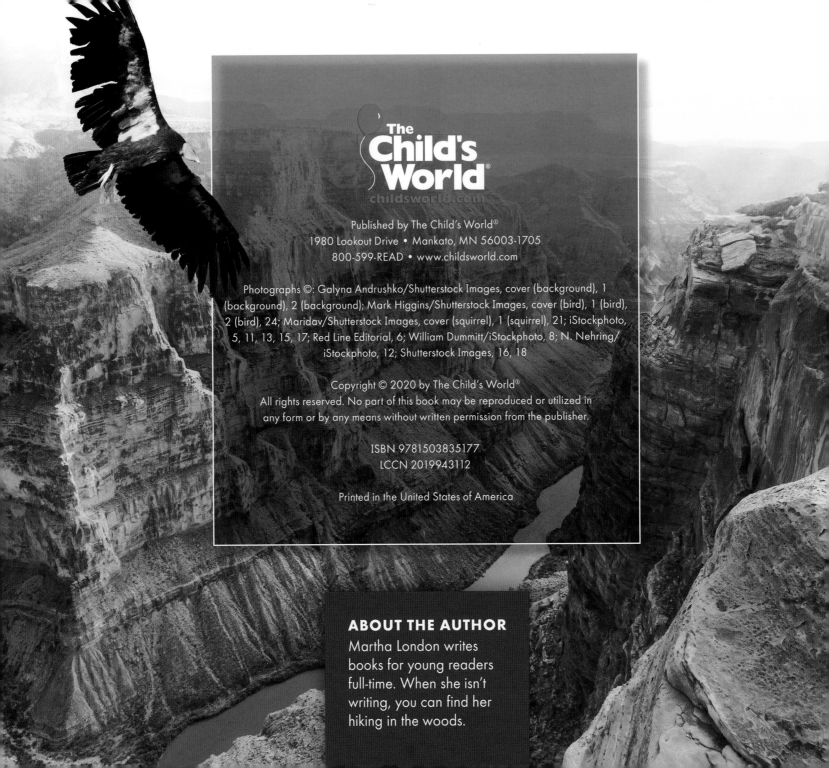

The Child's World®
childsworld.com

Published by The Child's World®
1980 Lookout Drive • Mankato, MN 56003-1705
800-599-READ • www.childsworld.com

Photographs ©: Galyna Andrushko/Shutterstock Images, cover (background), 1 (background), 2 (background); Mark Higgins/Shutterstock Images, cover (bird), 1 (bird), 2 (bird), 24; Maridav/Shutterstock Images, cover (squirrel), 1 (squirrel), 21; iStockphoto, 5, 11, 13, 15, 17; Red Line Editorial, 6; William Dummitt/iStockphoto, 8; N. Nehring/iStockphoto, 12; Shutterstock Images, 16, 18

ISBN 9781503835177
LCCN 2019943112

Printed in the United States of America

ABOUT THE AUTHOR
Martha London writes books for young readers full-time. When she isn't writing, you can find her hiking in the woods.

TABLE OF CONTENTS

CHAPTER ONE

The Grand Canyon's Layers

The Grand Canyon in Arizona is 277 miles (446 km) long. It has walls that are more than 6,000 feet (1,800 m) high. People come from all over the world to see the Grand Canyon. The walls of the canyon are striped. These stripes are layers of rock. The Grand Canyon has nearly 40 distinct layers. Many people find the layers beautiful. But the layers also help scientists.

The Grand Canyon's layers are like a timeline of Earth's history. Over many millions of years, layers of rock formed in the area where the Grand Canyon is today. In the last several million years, the Grand Canyon's steep walls were carved out. The walls show the stacked rock layers. The layers hold clues about what Earth was like when each layer formed. Scientists study the layers to learn how this area of Earth has changed over time.

More than six million people visited the Grand Canyon in 2018.

Layers of the Grand Canyon

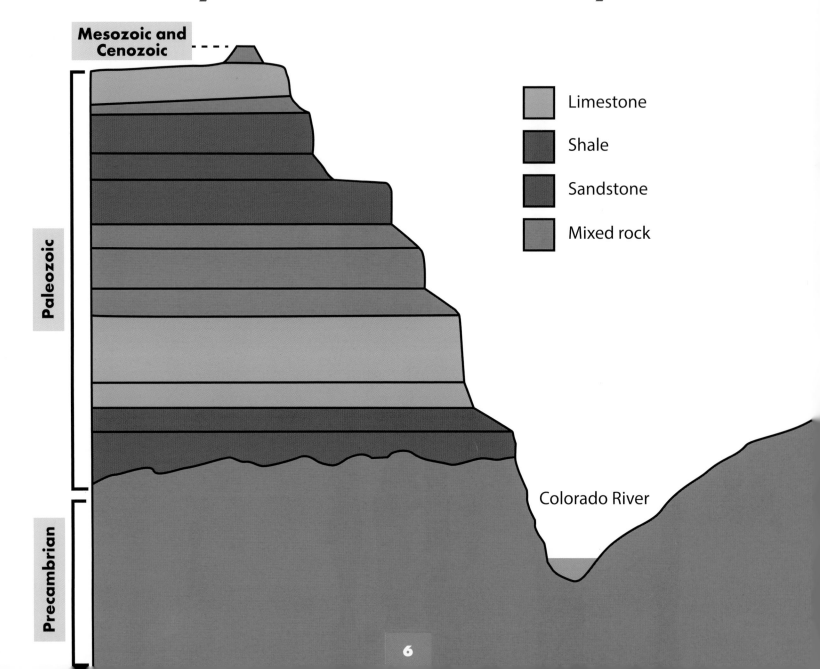

Mesozoic and Cenozoic

Paleozoic

Precambrian

Limestone

Shale

Sandstone

Mixed rock

Colorado River

The oldest layers of the Grand Canyon are at the bottom. Each layer is younger than the one below it. The youngest layers are at the top. Scientists divide the layers into four time periods. The oldest section is from the Precambrian (pree-KAM-bree-uhn) Era. The second-oldest section is the Paleozoic (pay-lee-uh-ZOH-ik) Era. It has many **fossils**. The youngest sections are the Mesozoic (meh-zuh-ZOH-ik) and Cenozoic (see-nuh-ZOH-ik) Eras. They mark the top of the Grand Canyon. The canyon was carved during the Cenozoic Era.

Wind, rain, and the flow of the Colorado River cause **erosion**. Erosion formed the walls of the canyon over millions of years. Because of erosion, the Grand Canyon continues to change.

The rocks at the bottom of the Grand Canyon are called basement rocks.

CHAPTER TWO

The Precambrian Era

T he oldest layers of the Grand Canyon were formed during the Precambrian Era. The Precambrian Era lasted for billions of years. It started when Earth was first formed. It ended about four billion years later. This was when life-forms with more than one cell came to be. Scientists have found fossils from the Precambrian Era in the Grand Canyon.

At the bottom of the Grand Canyon, some rocks are nearly two billion years old. This part of the canyon is made of very hard rocks. Layers of granite and sandstone make up most of this section. Granite comes from volcanic activity. Sandstone is made of many tiny pieces of rock.

CHAPTER THREE

The Paleozoic Era

The Paleozoic Era began about 540 million years ago. During that era, the area of the Grand Canyon was covered by a large sea. The sea carried small pieces of rock. These pieces are called **sediment**. The sediment fell to the sea floor. It did this for 300 million years. This created layers.

Scientists study the layers. In some of the layers, scientists have found sea fossils. These fossils show what kinds of sea life existed during the Paleozoic Era. Coral, **trilobite**, and leaf fossils are found in the Grand Canyon.

Some of the oldest known trilobites have been found in the Grand Canyon.

SHELL FOSSIL

Finding Fossils

Scientists find different kinds of fossils in different layers. Fossils in older layers are simple. They look like sea sponges or jellyfish. Fossils in newer layers are more complex. Scientists study these fossils to learn how living things have changed over time.

This section of the canyon has the most layers. It is up to 5,000 feet (1,500 m) thick. Many different types of rock make up these layers. Some examples are limestone, shale, and sandstone. Each kind of rock erodes differently. Some erode more easily than others. This changes the way the canyon walls form.

Sandstone, limestone, and shale are all sedimentary rocks. That means they were formed when water or wind **deposited** small bits of rock. Over time, the pieces hardened together.

Sandstone is often very hard. Some limestone is also hard. Hard rocks erode more slowly. The slow erosion carves steep cliffs. Shale and other types of limestone are soft. They erode easily. When shale erodes, it splits in lines. This creates ledges on the walls of the canyon. Soft rocks also erode into slopes.

Some of the Grand Canyon's cliffs, such as those of Redwall Cavern, are made of limestone.

CHAPTER FOUR

The Mesozoic Era

A round 250 million years ago, the Paleozoic Era ended. The Mesozoic Era began. The rock layers from this era are at the top of the Grand Canyon. But most of the Mesozoic rock is missing. The newest rock from this era is close to 250 million years old. This rock is from the beginning of the era.

There are only a few formations from the Mesozoic Era at the Grand Canyon. One is Cedar Mountain. Cedar Mountain is on the South Rim of the canyon. It shows what the canyon may have looked like millions of years ago. Scientists have concluded that the canyon used to be 4,000 to 8,000 feet (1,200 to 2,400 m) higher.

The remaining Mesozoic rocks are near the South Rim of the Grand Canyon.

Scientists are not sure why there are so few Mesozoic formations. They believe there could be two possible reasons. One is that not much sediment was deposited. The Mesozoic Era may have had less sea activity. This could have caused less sediment to be dropped onto the area.

CEDAR MOUNTAIN

Cedar Mountain is a butte, a steep hill with a flat top.

The other possibility is that there was a period of quick erosion. This erosion carried the newer rocks away. All that was left were smaller formations such as Cedar Mountain.

The Colorado River eroded much of the Grand Canyon.

LAVA FLOWS

Lava flows show researchers when certain parts of the canyon were carved.

CHAPTER FIVE

The Cenozoic Era

The Cenozoic Era began about 65 million years ago. It continues today. There are few Cenozoic Era features at the Grand Canyon. One Cenozoic feature is the lava flows. The Cenozoic Era had volcanic activity for millions of years. As the lava flowed down the canyon walls, it stopped where the bottom of the canyon was. Today, some of those flows are high up on the canyon.

The Grand Canyon itself was carved during the Cenozoic Era. Five to six million years ago, long periods of erosion occurred. The erosion shaped the canyon. The Grand Canyon got its distinct shape because of the area's dry **climate**. Dry climates have fewer plants. Plants help keep sediment in place. The Grand Canyon does not have a lot of plant life. This means that erosion happens easily.

The Colorado River is responsible for much of the canyon's erosion. The Colorado River flows at the bottom of the canyon. The river is fed by melting snow. As the water rushes through the canyon walls, it takes sediment with it. The Colorado River is a fast river. It carries a lot of sediment. Over time, the river easily carved downward through the sedimentary rock of the canyon walls. Because of the rapid erosion, the canyon deepened more quickly than it widened. This resulted in the magnificent canyon people see today.

FAST FACTS

- The Grand Canyon has nearly 40 distinct layers.

- The Grand Canyon's layers are divided into four eras: Precambrian, Paleozoic, Mesozoic, and Cenozoic.

- The oldest layers of rock are at the bottom of the canyon. The youngest are at the top.

- The oldest rocks are nearly two billion years old.

- The area of the Grand Canyon was covered by a large sea during the Paleozoic Era.

- The Grand Canyon is made of different rocks, including granite, sandstone, limestone, and shale.

- Most formations from the Mesozoic Era are missing.

- The Colorado River eroded much of the Grand Canyon during the Cenozoic Era.

GLOSSARY

climate (KLY-mit) Climate is the usual weather in an area. The Grand Canyon has a dry climate.

deposited (dee-POZ-it-ed) Deposited means to have let something fall to the ground. Water deposited sediment on the seafloor.

erosion (i-ROH-zhun) Erosion is the slow process of wearing away by water and wind. The Colorado River caused much of the Grand Canyon's erosion.

fossils (FOSS-uhlz) Fossils are the remains of a plant or animal from millions of years ago preserved in rock. Scientists found leaf fossils in the Grand Canyon.

sediment (SED-uh-muhnt) Sediment is tiny pieces of rock, sand, or dirt that have been carried away by water or wind. The sea carried the sediment.

trilobite (TRY-luh-bite) A trilobite is a sea creature from millions of years ago that was similar to today's insects and crabs. Scientists found trilobite fossils in the Grand Canyon.

TO LEARN MORE

IN THE LIBRARY

Chin, Jason. *Grand Canyon*. New York, NY: Roaring Book Press, 2017.

Gregory, Josh. *Grand Canyon*. New York, NY: Scholastic, 2018.

Mattern, Joanne. *The Grand Canyon: This Place Rocks*. South Egremont, MA: Red Chair Press, 2018.

ON THE WEB

Visit our website for links about the Grand Canyon:

childsworld.com/links

Note to Parents, Teachers, and Librarians: We routinely verify our Web links to make sure they are safe and active sites. So encourage your readers to check them out!

INDEX